Key
Bible
People
made easy

Mark Water

W9-BIN-391

HENDRICKSON
PUBLISHERS

Key Bible People Made Easy
Hendrickson Publishers, Inc.
P.O. Box 3473
Peabody, Massachusetts 01961-3473

Designed and produced
by Tony Cantale Graphics

First printing — September 2003

Manufactured in Hong Kong/China

Photography supplied by
Todd Bolen, Digital Stock, Digital
Vision, Foxx Photos, C Moore,
Photodisc and Tony Cantale

Illustrations by
Tony Cantale Graphics

Contents

Pullout chart

Seven people who were helped by Jesus.

Adam and Eve

Adam

Meaning of name: Mankind

Point of interest: The first person created by God.

Family links: Adam was Eve's husband. His children were Cain, Abel, and Seth.

New Testament link: "Therefore, just as sin entered the world through one man, and death through sin, and in this way death came to all men, because all sinned." *Romans 5:12*

Quote: "I heard you in the garden, and I was afraid because I was naked; so I hid." *Genesis 3:10*

Link to Jesus: As Adam was the head of the human race, so Jesus was the Head of the new creation: *Romans 5:12-14; 1 Corinthians 15:21,22,45; Galatians 3:22,26; Ephesians 1:22,23.*

Key verse: Speaking to the serpent, the Lord God foretells the long conflict between the children of God and the children of evil. This is the first reference in the Bible to the salvation which Jesus brought. Jesus is the One who will crush the serpent's head, that is defeat evil. "And I will put enmity between you and the woman, and between your offspring and hers; he will crush your head, and you will strike his heel." *Genesis 3:15*

More Information: *Genesis 1:26,27; 2:1–5:5*

4

The result of Adam's sin

The New Testament shows how Jesus deals with the results of Adam's sin.

	Adam's sin		New Testament
1.	*Genesis 3:8,9*	Separation	*Mark 15:34*
2.	*Genesis 3:16*	Pain	*Acts 2:24*
3.	*Genesis 3:17*	God's curse	*Galatians 3:13*
4.	*Genesis 3:17*	Sorrow	*Matthew 27:29*
5.	*Genesis 3:18*	Thorns	*Mark 15:17*
6.	*Genesis 3:19*	Sweat	*Luke 22:44*
7.	*Genesis 3:19*	Death	*Philippians 2:8*

Eve

Meaning of name: Life

Point of interest: Eve was the first woman God created.

Family links: Eve was Adam's wife. Her children were Cain, Abel, and Seth.

New Testament link: "But I am afraid that just as Eve was deceived by the serpent's cunning, your minds may somehow be led astray from your sincere and pure devotion to Christ." *2 Corinthians 11:3*

Quote: "The serpent deceived me and I ate." *Genesis 3:13*

Link to Jesus: To her cost, Eve discovered that Satan was a liar. The serpent said to Eve, "Did God really say, 'You must not eat from any tree in the garden'?" *Genesis 3:1*. In *John 8:44*, Jesus says of the devil, "he is a liar and the father of lies."

Key verse: "She [Eve] took some [fruit of the tree] and ate it." *Genesis 3:6*

More Information: *Genesis 2:18–3:20*

The Temptation of Adam and Eve, façade, Milan Cathedral, Italy

Eve and temptation

Just as Eve was tempted in three ways, so we are tempted today. *See Genesis 3:6.*

1. **Temptation comes through our eyes:** Eve saw the fruit.
2. **Temptation comes through our desires:** Eve desired the fruit.
3. **Temptation comes as a result of our actions:** Eve took the fruit.

"In Adam", but also "in Christ"

The apostle Paul speaks of Christians as being "in Adam" as well as being "in Christ." "For as in Adam all die, so in Christ all will be made alive." *1 Corinthians 15:22*

Before we become Christians, we are "in Adam" in that we are rooted in sin.

But as Christians, we are "in Christ" and related to Jesus, forgiven of our sin and renewed with his spiritual life.

Cain and Abel

Cain and Abel

Meaning of names: "Cain" means "acquire"; "Abel" means "shepherd."

Point of interest: Cain murdered Abel.

Family links: Cain and Abel were sons of Adam and Eve.

New Testament link: "By faith Abel offered God a better sacrifice than Cain did. By faith he was commended as a righteous man, when God spoke well of his offerings. And by faith he still speaks, even though he is dead." *Hebrews 11:4*

Quote: Replying to God's question, "Where is your brother Abel?" Cain said, "Am I my brother's keeper?" *Genesis 4:9*

Key verse: "Then the Lord said to Cain, 'Why are you angry? Why is your face downcast? If you do what is right, will you not be accepted? But if you do not do what is right, sin is crouching at your door; it desires to have you, but you must master it.'" *Genesis 4:7*

More Information: *Genesis 4:1,2*

The first murder

Cain was Adam and Eve's eldest son. He farmed the land. God rejected Cain's sacrifice, but accepted Abel's animal sacrifice. Cain was so jealous and angry that he killed Abel in a field.

Job

Job

Meaning of name: Persecuted

Point of interest: Job endured terrible, undeserved suffering.

Family links: Before he suffered Job had:

- 7 sons
- 3 daughters
- 7,000 sheep
- 3,000 camels
- 500 yoke of oxen
- 500 donkeys.

After he suffered God blessed Job with:

- 7 sons
- 3 daughters
- 14,000 sheep
- 6,000 camels
- 1,000 yoke of oxen
- 1,000 donkeys.

New Testament link: "You have heard of Job's perseverance." *James 5:11*

Quote: "I know that my Redeemer lives." *Job 19:25*

Link to Jesus: Job endured suffering, in which he was patient, and from which he was delivered.

Key verse: Job said: "But he [God] knows the way that I take; when he has tested me, I shall come forth as gold." *Job 23:10*

More Information: The book of *Job*

Job as an example of righteousness

The prophet Ezekiel mentions Job, along with Noah and Daniel, as an example of righteousness in *Ezekiel 14:14*.

"I despise myself"

The opening verse of the book of Job characterizes Job as someone who was "blameless and upright, who feared God and shunned evil." But at the end of the book Job says of himself: "I despise myself and repent in dust and ashes." *Job 42:6*

The more we grow in the grace of God, the more we realize that we are only sinners saved by God's grace.

Enoch and Methuselah

Enoch

Meaning of name: Teacher

Point of interest: Enoch was one of only two people (the other being Elijah in 2 Kings 2:11) whom the Bible says were "translated" to heaven, into the presence of God, without dying.

Family links: Enoch's father was Jared. Enoch was the father of Methuselah.

New Testament link: "By faith Enoch was taken from this life, so that he did not experience death; he could not be found, because God had taken him away. For before he was taken, he was commended as one who pleased God." *Hebrews 11:5*

Key verse: "Enoch walked with God; then he was no more, because God took him away." *Genesis 5:24*

More Information: Genesis 5:18-24

Walking with God

"Walking with God" is a picture of having close fellowship with God.

"Noah was a righteous man, ... and he walked with God." *Genesis 6:9*

"And what does the Lord require of you? To act justly and to love mercy and to walk humbly with your God." *Micah 6:8*

"True instruction was found in his mouth and nothing false was found on his lips. He walked with me in peace and uprightness, and turned many from sin." *Malachi 2:6*

Methuselah

Meaning of name: Man of the javelin

Point of interest: Methuselah was the oldest person to have lived. He died when he was 969 .

Family links: His father was Enoch, and he was the father of Lamech, and grandfather of Noah.

New Testament link: In Luke's genealogy of Jesus, Methuselah is mentioned: " ... the son of Methuselah, the son of Enoch ..." *Luke 3:37*

Key verse: In Genesis 5:25,26 Methuselah is mentioned, and is the eighth patriarch listed in this chapter.

More Information: Genesis 5:21-27; Luke 3:37

Noah

Noah

Meaning of name: Rest

Point of interest: Noah was a "preacher of righteousness." See *2 Peter 2:5*

Family links: Noah had three sons: Shem, Japheth, and Ham.

New Testament link: "By faith Noah, when warned about things not yet seen, in holy fear built an ark to save his family. By his faith he condemned the world and became heir of the righteousness that comes by faith." *Hebrews 11:7*

Words spoken about: "Noah was a righteous man, blameless among the people of his time, and he walked with God." *Genesis 6:9*

Link to Jesus: Noah prepared the way of salvation: *Genesis 6:14; Hebrews 11:7*
Noah finished God's work: *Genesis 6:22; John 19:30*

Key verse: "Noah did everything just as God commanded him." *Genesis 7:22*

More Information: *Genesis 5–9; Luke 3:36; 1 Peter 3:20; 2 Peter 2:5*

The sign of the rainbow

After the flood God made a promise to Noah for all time: he would never again send a flood to destroy all living things. God gave the rainbow as a sign of that promise. See *Genesis 9:11-17*.

Rainbows are very significant in the Bible. They announce God's judgments in a vivid, pictorial way:

- "Like the appearance of a rainbow in the clouds on a rainy day, so was the radiance around him." *Ezekiel 1:28*.

- "Then I saw another mighty angel coming down from heaven. He was robed in a cloud, with a rainbow above his head ..." *Revelation 10:1*.

Abraham

Abraham

Meaning of name: Father of multitudes. Abraham was also called "Abram"

Point of interest: Abraham was the founder of the Jewish nation.

Family links: Abraham's father was Terah, his nephew was Lot, his wife was Sarah (Sarai), and his son was Isaac.

New Testament link: Jesus claimed to have existed before Abraham's time. "'I tell you the truth,' Jesus answered, 'before Abraham was born, I am!'" *John 8:58*

Quote: "God himself will provide the lamb for the burnt offering, my son." *Genesis 22:8*

Link to Jesus:
- Abraham expressed his concerns freely, and with great faith, in his prayer life. "Abraham said, 'O Sovereign Lord, what can you give me since I remain childless? . . . You have given me no children.'" *Genesis 15:2,3*
- In all the critical moments of his life Abraham prayed to God. See *Genesis 18:16-33; 20:7*.

Key verse: "Abram believed the Lord, and he credited it to him as righteousness." *Genesis 15:6*

More Information: *Genesis 11:1–25:11; Matthew 1:1,2; Acts 7:2,3; Hebrews 11:8-19*

By faith

The book of Hebrews gives a summary of Abraham's wonderful life of faith.

"By faith Abraham, when called to go to a place he would later receive as his inheritance, obeyed and went, even though he did not know where he was going.

"By faith he made his home in the promised land like a stranger in a foreign country; he lived in tents, as did Isaac and Jacob, who were heirs with him of the same promise. For he was looking forward to the city with foundations, whose architect and builder is God.

"By faith Abraham, even though he was past age – and Sarah herself was barren – was enabled to become a father because he considered him faithful who had made the promise. And so from this one man, and he as good as dead, came descendants as numerous as the stars in the sky and as countless as the sand on the seashore.

"All these people were still living by faith when they died. They did not receive the things promised; they only saw them and welcomed them from a distance. And they admitted that they were aliens and strangers on earth.

"People who say such things

show that they are looking for a country of their own. If they had been thinking of the country they had left, they would have had opportunity to return.

"Instead, they were longing for a better country – a heavenly one. Therefore God is not ashamed to be called their God, for he has prepared a city for them.

"By faith Abraham, when God tested him, offered Isaac as a sacrifice. He who had received the promises was about to sacrifice his one and only son, even though God had said to him, 'It is through Isaac that your offspring will be reckoned.' Abraham reasoned that God could raise the dead, and figuratively speaking, he did receive Isaac back from death."
Hebrews 11:8-19

Summary of life
Abraham lived around 2000 BC. He grew up in the prosperous town of Ur in Mesopotamia.
- God called Abraham to leave Ur and to set off into the unknown. He then lived in Haran, before he traveled to Canaan.
- Abraham believed God's promise that a great nation would descend from him, even though Sarah was past the age of child-bearing.
- After his son Isaac was born, Abraham showed his faith and obedience to God by being prepared to sacrifice Isaac.

Melchizedek

Melchizedek

Meaning of name: King of righteousness

Point of interest: Melchizedek was a mysterious king of Salem (Jerusalem) to whom Abraham paid a tithe.

Family links: Melchizedek was said to be, "Without father or mother, without genealogy, without beginning of days or end of life …" *Hebrews 7:3*

New Testament link: According to *Hebrews 7:3*, Melchizedek, "like the Son of God he remains a priest forever."

Quote: Melchizedek blessed Abram, saying, "Blessed be Abram by God Most High, Creator of heaven and earth. And blessed be God Most High, who delivered your enemies into your hand." *Genesis 14:19,20*

Link to Jesus: Melchizedek, the priest-king, *Genesis 14:18-20*, is a type of the priesthood of Jesus, *Hebrews 6:20; 7:1-17,24,25.*

Key verse: "Jesus … has become a high priest forever, in the order of Melchizedek." *Hebrews 6:20*

More Information: *Genesis 14:18-20; Psalm 110:4; Hebrews 5:6; 7:3*

King and priest

Melchizedek was king of Salem (Jerusalem). He was also priest of the most high God, and he blessed Abraham.

Melchizedek is a prophetic symbol of Jesus who was both King and Priest.

Isaac

Isaac

Meaning of name: Laughing
Point of interest: Being the second of the patriarchs of the Israelites.
Family links: Isaac's very elderly parents were Sarah and Abraham. Isaac's bride, Rebekah, was found by Abraham's faithful servant. Isaac and Rebekah had twins, Jacob and Esau.
New Testament link: Isaac is referred to as a son of promise in *Romans 4:16-21; 9:7-9*.
Words spoken to: At Beersheba, the Lord said to Isaac, "I am the God of your father Abraham. Do not be afraid, for I am with you; I will bless you and will increase the number of your descendants for the sake of my servant Abraham." *Genesis 26:24*
Key verse: "Was not our ancestor Abraham considered righteous for what he did when he offered his son Isaac on the altar?" *James 2:21*
More Information: *Genesis 21:1–28:9; 35:27-29; Matthew 1:2*

13

The ram

God ordered Abraham to sacrifice his son Isaac. As he raised his knife to kill his tied up son, the angel of the LORD called out, "Abraham, Abraham."

Abraham replied, "Here I am."

"'Do not lay a hand on the boy,' he said. 'Do not do anything to him. Now I know that you fear God, because you have not withheld from me your son, your only son.'" *Genesis 22:12*

Then Abraham saw a ram caught in a thicket, which he sacrificed in place of Isaac. The idea of Jesus as our substitute is detailed in *Hebrews 10:5-10*.

An unexpected blessing

In Isaac's old age, when he was nearly blind, he was tricked into blessing Jacob with the blessing that was rightly Esau's. But the New Testament even looks at this through the eyes of faith.

"Isaac blessed Jacob and Esau in regard to their future." *Hebrews 11:20*

Joseph and his brothers

Joseph

Meaning of name: Increaser

Point of interest: His coat of "many colors." This was a richly ornamented coat that had long sleeves. It was given to the heir in a family. So it was hardly surprising that Joseph's brothers were mad with jealousy when Jacob gave Joseph, the youngest but one in the family, this coat.

Family links: Joseph was Rachel's first son, but Jacob's eleventh son. Joseph had one brother and ten half-brothers.
Joseph and Asenath, daughter of Potiphera, priest of On, had two sons, Ephraim and Manasseh.

New Testament link: "By faith Joseph, when his end was near, spoke about the exodus of the Israelites from Egypt and gave instructions about his bones." *Hebrews 11:22*

Quote: "I am your brother Joseph, the one you sold into Egypt! *Genesis 45:4*

Link to Jesus: Joseph is seen to be a type of Jesus in many ways:
- Joseph was stripped of his coat/robe. Compare *Genesis 37:23* with *John 19:23, 24.*
- Joseph was sold for the price of a slave. Compare *Genesis 37:28* with *Matthew 26:15.*
- Joseph was taken into Egypt. Compare *Genesis 37:24* with *Matthew 2:14, 15.*
- Joseph was falsely accused. Compare *Genesis 39:16-18* with *Matthew 26:59, 60.*
- Joseph was placed with two prisoners, one of whom was delivered and one of whom was lost. Compare *Genesis 40: 2,3,21,23* with *Luke 23:32,33,39-43.*
- Joseph started his ministry, aged 30. Compare *Genesis 41:46* with *Luke 3:23.*
- Joseph became a blessing to Gentile nations. Compare *Genesis 45:46-57* with *John 1:12.*

Key verse: "You intended to harm me, but God intended it for good to accomplish what is now being done, the saving of many lives." *Genesis 50:20*

More Information: *Genesis 30:20-24; 37–50*

Joseph's eventful life

After his two significant dreams Joseph was sold by his brothers as a slave and ended up in Egypt. There Joseph became the steward in the home of a leading soldier, Potiphar.

- Joseph was falsely accused of having sex with Potiphar's wife and so was thrown into prison.
- Joseph was released from prison, interpreted the king of Egypt's dreams, and on the strength of that was made the equivalent of vice-president of Egypt.

Through Joseph, Jacob's family was saved from the terrible seven-year-long famine. Joseph's family had to settle in Egypt where Joseph looked after them.

Learning from Joseph's life

- Joseph's refusal to be seduced by Potiphar's wife is admirable. Joseph reasoned, "No one is greater in this house than I am. My master has withheld nothing from me except you, because you are his wife. How then could I do such a wicked thing and sin against God?" *Genesis 39:9*
- Later when Potiphar's wife approached Joseph again, Joseph took evasive action and ran out of the house. See *Genesis 39:11,12.*

Crops being assessed for taxing. Egyptian tomb painting from around 1400 BC.

Moses

Moses

Meaning of name: Drawer out

Point of interest: Moses led the Israelites out of their slavery in Egypt, after the ten terrible plagues, into the desert, where God gave him the Ten Commandments.

Family links: Moses had one sister, Miriam, and one brother Aaron. Moses was brought up in the king of Egypt's palace because an Egyptian princess found the baby Moses, hidden in a basket among the reeds of the River Nile.

After Moses had killed a cruel Egyptian taskmaster, he was forced to flee from Egypt. He found refuge in the desert with Jethro, whose daughter, Zipporah, Moses married. They had two sons, Gershom, *Exodus 2:22; 18:3,* and Eliezer, *Exodus 18:4.* Moses named his children after events he experienced in his life. "Gershom" sounds like the Hebrew for "an alien here." Moses said, "I have become an alien in a foreign land."

"Eliezer" means "my God is helper." Moses said, "My father's God was my helper; he saved me from the sword of Pharaoh."

New Testament link: "Moses was faithful in all God's house." *Hebrews 3:2*

Quote: "You will see the deliverance the Lord will bring you today." *Exodus 14:13*

Link to Jesus: Jesus himself used the example of the bronze snake Moses put on a pole in the desert, *Numbers 21:6-9,* which saved anyone who looked to it in faith from dying of a snake bite. Jesus used it as a picture of his own resurrection.

"Just as Moses lifted up the snake in the desert, so the Son of Man must be lifted up, that everyone who believes in him may have eternal life." *John 3:14,15*

Key verse: "There the angel of the Lord appeared to him in flames of fire from within a bush. Moses saw that though the bush was on fire it did not burn up." *Exodus 3:2*

More Information: The complete books of *Exodus, Leviticus, Numbers,* and *Deuteronomy,* and *Luke 9:28-36; Hebrews 11:23-29*

By faith Moses ...

The writer of the letter to the Hebrews does not think of the events in Moses' life as mere secular history. He saw them as instances of how Moses lived his courageous life of faith.

"By faith Moses' parents hid him for three months after he was born, because they saw he was no ordinary child, and they were not afraid of the king's edict.

By faith Moses, when he had grown up, refused to be known as the son of Pharaoh's daughter. He chose to be mistreated along with the people of God rather than to enjoy the pleasures of sin for a short time. He regarded disgrace for the sake of Christ as of greater value than the treasures of Egypt, because he was looking ahead to his reward. By faith he left Egypt, not fearing the king's anger; he persevered because he saw him who is invisible. By faith he kept the Passover and the sprinkling of blood, so that the destroyer of the firstborn would not touch the firstborn of Israel.

By faith the people passed through the Red Sea as on dry land; but when the Egyptians tried to do so, they were drowned." *Hebrews 11:23-29*

The tabernacle

In the desert God gave Moses very detailed instructions about how the Israelites were to worship him. The portable tent, known as the tabernacle, was erected for the sole purpose of worshiping God.

"Then have them make a sanctuary for me, and I will dwell among them. Make this tabernacle and all its furnishings exactly like the pattern I will show you." *Exodus 25:8,9*

The writer to the Hebrews explains that the tabernacle has a most important spiritual meaning, which has been surpassed and fulfilled in Jesus.

"For Christ did not enter a man-made sanctuary that was only a copy of the true one; he entered heaven itself, now to appear for us in God's presence." *Hebrews 9:24*

Joshua

Joshua

Meaning of name: God is salvation
Point of interest: Joshua led the people of Israel into the Promised Land.
Family links: Joshua was the son of Nun.
New Testament link: "By faith the walls of Jericho fell, after the people had marched around them for seven days." *Hebrews 11:30*
Words spoken to: "Be strong and courageous. Do not be terrified; do not be discouraged, for the Lord your God will be with you wherever you go." *Joshua 1:9*
Key verse: "But as for me and my household, we will serve the Lord." *Joshua 24:15*
More Information: *Exodus 17:9-13; 24:13; Numbers 13–14;* the whole book of *Joshua*

Characteristics of Joshua

- Joshua was both a military and a spiritual leader.
- In the wilderness Joshua was Moses' right hand man.
- With Caleb, Joshua spied out the land of Canaan and encouraged the Israelites to attack it. He said that with God's help they could conquer the land.
- After Moses' death Joshua became the leader of the Israelites and led them into the Promised Land.

Rahab

"Rahab" means "broad." Rahab had been a prostitute, *Joshua 2:1.* But she later served God very faithfully and hid two of Joshua's spies. As a result of this when Jericho was captured by Joshua, "Rahab, her father and mother and all who belonged to her" were spared. See *Joshua 6:23.*

The letter to the Hebrews commends Rahab for acting out of faith in God:

"By faith the prostitute Rahab, because she welcomed the spies, was not killed with those who were disobedient." *Hebrews 11:31*

Ruth

Ruth

Meaning of name: Companion

Point of interest: Ruth was faithful to her mother-in-law, Naomi, and returning with her to Bethlehem, where Ruth met a relative of Naomi's, Boaz, and married him.

Family links: Ruth's son, Obed, was the father of Jesse, whose son was King David.

New Testament link: Matthew includes Ruth's name in his genealogy of Jesus, in *Matthew 1:5.*

Quote: "Don't urge me to leave you or to turn back from you. Where you go I will go, and where you stay I will stay. Your people will be my people and your God my God." *Ruth 1:16*

Key verse: "The woman said to Naomi: 'Praise be to the Lord who this day has not left you without a kinsman-redeemer.'" *Ruth 4:14*

More Information: The whole of the book of *Ruth; Matthew 1:5.*

Naomi

Naomi had:
- lost her husband, *Ruth 1:3*
- lost her sons, *Ruth 1:5*
- lost her joy, *Ruth 1:20*

But, through the faithfulness of Ruth and the generosity of Boaz, Naomi's joy was restored after she returned to Bethlehem.

"Then Naomi took the child; laid him in her lap and cared for him. The women living there said, 'Naomi has a son.'" *Ruth 4:16*

Gideon

Gideon

Meaning of name: Great warrior

Point of interest: Gideon, Israel's fifth judge and ruler, defeated the Midianites and the Amalekites — semi-nomadic peoples — and so gave the Israelites 30 years of peace.

Family links: Gideon's father was Joash. Gideon's two named sons were Jether and Abimelech. Gideon "had seventy sons of his own, for he had many wives." *Judges 8:30*

New Testament link: Gideon is only mentioned once in the New Testament. The book of Hebrews says that Gideon lived a life of faith in God. "And what more shall I say? I do not have time to tell about Gideon, Barak, Samson, Jephthah, David, Samuel and the prophets, who through faith conquered kingdoms, administered justice, and gained what was promised; who shut the mouths of lions, quenched the fury of the flames, and escaped the edge of the sword; whose weakness was turned to strength; and who became powerful in battle and routed foreign armies." *Hebrews 11:32-34*

Quote: "When I and all who are with me blow our trumpets, then from all around the camp blow yours and shout, 'For the Lord and for Gideon.'" *Judges 7:18*

Link to Jesus: Gideon was the fifth judge of the Israelites. He brought Israel back into fellowship with God by smashing his father's statue of Baal. Jesus, our advocate, brings us back into fellowship with God, as we confess our sins and ask for his forgiveness. See *1 John 1:7, 9; 2:1.*

Key verse: "The Lord said to Gideon, 'With the three hundred men that lapped I will save you and give the Midianites into your hands.'" *Judges 7:7*

More Information: *Judges 6–8*

Samson

Samson

Meaning of name: Distinguished
Point of interest: His physical strength.
Family links: Samson's father was
Manoah. Samson's mother, who is not
named, had been sterile and so was
childless. But an angel appeared to
her and told her that she would
conceive and give birth to a son.
Samson's parents were told that their
child would be especially dedicated to
God as a Nazirite who would save the
Israelites from the Philistines.
See *Judges 13:1-24.*
Samson married a Philistine woman
from Timnah, whom the Philistines
killed. Samson later fell in love with
another Philistine, Delilah. Samson
died childless.
New Testament link: Apart from a
fleeting mention in *Hebrews 11:32,*
Samson is not mentioned in the New
Testament.
Quote: "'No razor has ever been used
on my head,' he said, 'because I have
been a Nazirite set apart to God since
birth. If my head were shaved, my
strength would leave me, and I would
become as weak as any other man.'"
Judges 16:17
Key verse: As a blinded prisoner,
Samson's last prayer, just before he
pulled down the Philistine temple on
the Philistines and on himself was:
"'O Sovereign Lord, remember me. O
God, please strengthen me just once
more, and let me with one blow get
revenge on the Philistines for my two
eyes.'" *Judges 16:28*
More Information: *Judges 13–16*

21

Samson's riddle

Samson gave the Philistines
this riddle to solve. If they
could not solve it they had to
give him 30 linen garments
and thirty sets of clothes.

> "Out of the eater, something
>   to eat;
> out of the strong, something
>   sweet."
> *Judges 14:14*

The answer to the riddle and
what happened when the
Philistines gave Samson the
right answer is in *Judges
14:12-20.*

Samson destroys the Philistine temple: Gustav Doré.

Samuel

Samuel

Meaning of name: Asked of God

Point of interest: Samuel was the last great warrior-judge of Israel, and one of their first prophets.

Family links: Samuel's parents were Hannah and Elkanah. He was born in answer to Hannah's prayers. Like his mentor Eli, Samuel was unable to influence his sons to lead a godly life. See *1 Samuel 8:3*.

New Testament link: Acts 3:24 views Samuel as the first of the prophets. Samuel was the last of the judges: "After this, God gave them judges until the time of Samuel the prophet." *Acts 13:20*

Quote: "As for me, far be it from me that I should sin against the Lord by failing to pray for you." *1 Samuel 12:23*

Key verse: Samuel's final act was to anoint David, privately, to be the next king of Israel. "So Samuel took the horn of oil and anointed him [David] in the presence of his brothers, and from that day on the Spirit of the Lord came upon David in power." *1 Samuel 16:13*

More Information: 1 Samuel 1–4; 7–16

Samuel's understanding compared with teaching in the New Testament

- Samuel told Saul that the Lord had looked for a man after God's own heart (David), and had appointed him leader of his people. Compare *1 Samuel 13:14* with *Acts 13:21, 22*.

- Samuel knew that to obey is better than sacrifice. Compare *1 Samuel 15:22* with *Mark 12:23*.

- Samuel knew that the Lord does not look on the outward appearance of a person. Compare *1 Samuel 16:7* with *2 Corinthians 10:7*.

Saul

Saul

Meaning of name: Asked

Point of interest: Saul was the first king of Israel.

Family links: Saul was son of Kish. His wives were Ahinoam and Rizpah. His children were Jonathan, Malki-Shua, Abinadab, Esh-baal (Ish-Bosheth), Armoni, Mephibosheth, Merab, Michal.

New Testament link: King Saul is not mentioned in the New Testament.

Quote: "As they danced, they sang: 'Saul has slain his thousands, and David his tens of thousands.' Saul was very angry; this refrain galled him. 'They have credited David with tens of thousands,' he thought, 'but me with only thousands. What more can he get but the kingdom?' And from that time on Saul kept a jealous eye on David." *1 Samuel 18:7-9*

Key verse: At the end of his life Saul consulted the witch of Endor. "So Saul disguised himself, putting on other clothes, and at night he and two men went to the woman. 'Consult a spirit for me,' he said, 'and bring up for me the one I name.'" *1 Samuel 28:8*

More Information: *1 Samuel 8–31; 2 Samuel 1*

The decline and fall of Saul

There are more things in Saul's life to avoid than to follow. Self-will and stubbornness were two characteristics that marred Saul's life. See *1 Samuel 15:19-23.* Saul's sin is:

- forbidden by God: see *2 Chronicles 30:8; Psalm 95:8*
- unbelief: see *2 Kings 7:14*
- pride: see *Nehemiah 9:16,29*
- refusing to listen to God: see *Proverbs 1:24*
- an evil heart: see *Jeremiah 7:24*
- rebelling against God: see *Psalm 78:8*
- resisting God's Spirit: see *Acts 7:51.*

David

David

Meaning of name: Beloved

Point of interest: David was Israel's second and greatest king, who loved the Lord with all his heart.

Family links: David was the great-grandson of Ruth and Boaz, and son of Jesse, from the tribe of Judah. He was the youngest of eight brothers. Eight of David's wives are named: Michal, Ahinoam of Jezreel (their child Amnon), Abigail, widow of Nabal (Kileab or Daniel), Maacah (Absalom), Haggith (Adonijah), Abital (Shephatiah), Eglah (Ithream), Bathsheba (Shimea, Shobab, Nathan, Solomon). Ten other children whom David had by other wives are named: see *1 Chronicles 3:6-9; 14:3,4,* not to mention other sons from David's concubines: *1 Chronicles 3:9.*

New Testament link: David is listed as an ancestor of Jesus in the two family trees of Jesus in the New Testament. "David was the father of Solomon" *Matthew 1:6*; "... the son of David ..." *Luke 3:31*

Quote: After David's adultery with Bathsheba, he confessed his sin to God by saying, "Against you, you only, have I sinned and done what is evil in your sight." *Psalm 51:4*

Link to Jesus: In the Bible no one else is called David. This underlines the unique place David has as the ancestor, forerunner and foreshadower of the Lord Jesus Christ, who is great David's greater son. Jesus is repeatedly called "Son of David."

Paul says that Jesus "was a descendant of David." *Romans 1:3* Jesus himself is recorded by John as saying "'I am the Root and the Offspring of David.'" *Revelation 22:16*

Key verse: 73 of the psalms are said to be "David's" psalms. Jesus in Luke 20:42 spoke of David being the author of Psalm 110, from which he quotes to make clear how he was the Messiah. "The Lord says to my Lord: 'Sit at my right hand until I make your enemies a footstool for your feet.'" *Psalm 110:1*

More Information: The whole of *1 Samuel* and *2 Samuel; 1 Chronicles 11–29*

Goliath

"an exile" or "soothsayer"

Goliath, the Philistine champion, was over 9 feet tall. He was protected in heavy armor, and just the tip of his spear weighed 15 pounds.

- When the Israelites saw Goliath, they said that he was too big to defeat.
- When David saw Goliath, he said that he was too big to miss!

Bathsheba
"the seventh daughter"

The Bible holds up David as a spiritual giant. But it does not gloss over his faults and very serious sins. His most infamous failing came as a result of seeing Bathsheba taking her bath. Not only did he commit adultery with her, but he instigated the death of her husband, Uriah. Psalm 51 is David's great lament in which he pours out his heart to God, asking for his forgiveness.

The point about David's sins is that even though he committed them, he repented, so God was able to continue to use him in very special ways.

Absalom
"father of peace"

David greatly loved his son Absalom, but Absalom tried to steal the heart of the Israelites so he could gain his father's throne. He met his death in a most unusual way.

"Now Absalom happened to meet David's men. He was riding his mule, and as the mule went under the thick branches of a large oak, Absalom's head got caught in the tree. He was left hanging in mid-air, while the mule he was riding kept on going." *2 Samuel 18:9*

Joab and his men then killed Absalom.

Solomon
"Peace"

Solomon was the son of David and Bathsheba. Solomon succeeded David on Israel's throne. He build a magnificent temple in Jerusalem to honor the Lord.

Solomon used 30,000 men of Israel to transport cedar and pine logs from Lebanon.

"Solomon had seventy thousand carriers and eighty thousand stone-cutters in the hills, as well as thirty-three hundred foremen who supervised the project and directed the workmen." *1 Kings 5:15*

Elijah

Elijah

Meaning of name: The Lord is my God
Point of interest: His confrontation with the prophets of Baal on Mount Carmel.
Family links: Nothing is known about Elijah's family.
New Testament link: *Malachi 4:5,6* says that Elijah's ministry will be revived before the coming of the great and dreadful day of the Lord. Jesus said that this all applied to John the Baptist. See *Matthew 11:14; 17:11,12*
Elijah appeared in person when Jesus was transfigured. See *Mark 9:4*.

Quote: "'How long will you waver between two opinions? If the Lord is God, follow him; but if Baal is God, follow him.'" *1 Kings 18:21*
Key verse: Elijah was the greatest ecstatic prophet in the Old Testament and his Spirit-led actions often left people confused. "'But now you tell me to go to my master and say, "Elijah is here." I don't know where the Spirit of the Lord may carry you when I leave you. If I go and tell Ahab and he doesn't find you, he will kill me.'" *1 Kings 18:11,12*
More Information: *1 Kings 17–19; 2 Kings 1–2; Luke 4:25, 26; Romans 11:2-4; James 5:17,18*

The most prominent prophet

Elijah was the most prominent prophet of his time, 875–850 BC. He lived at a critical time in the history of Israel. The evil king, Ahab, married Jezebel who was the daughter of Ethbaal, king of Sidon. Jezebel persuaded Ahab to adopt the worship of Baal.

Elijah spent his energy in confronting Queen Jezebel and King Ahab as they attempted to draw the Israelites away from the worship of the one true God.

Prophets of Israel

Before Elijah and Elisha there were three prophets who prophesied to the northern kingdom of Israel: Ahijah, Iddo, and Jehu.

After Elijah and Elisha there were two prophets who prophesied to the kingdom of Israel: Amos and Hosea.

View from the top of Mount Carmel.

Elisha

Elisha

Meaning of name: God is Savior

Point of interest: Elisha was Elijah's disciple. He carryied on the prophetic work after watching Elijah being "translated" as he was caught up in a chariot of fire. Elisha performed 14 miracles, the most notable one being the curing of General Naaman of his leprosy.

Family links: Elisha's father was Shaphat.

New Testament link: *Luke 4:27* is the only New Testament reference to Elisha.

Quote: "Let me inherit a double portion of your spirit." *2 Kings 2:9*

Key verse: "The company of the prophets from Jericho, who were watching, said, 'The spirit of Elijah is resting on Elisha.'" *2 Kings 2:15*

More Information: *1 Kings 19:16,19-21; 2 Kings 2–9; 13:14-20*

Kings of Israel

After the Israelites split into two kingdoms, the northern kingdom of Israel was ruled by seventeen kings before it was captured by Assyria in 722 BC.

The kings of Israel were: Jeroboam I, Nadab, Baasha, Elah, Zimri, Omri, Ahab, Ahaziah, Jehoram, Jehu, Jehoahaz, Jehoash, Jeroboam II, Zechariah, Shallum, Manahem, Pekahiah, Pekah, and Hoshea.

Elijah and Elisha were prophets in the reigns of Ahab, Ahaziah, and Jehoram.

Isaiah

Isaiah

Meaning of name: Salvation of God

Point of interest: His call to be a prophet, recorded in *Isaiah 6:1-13*, when he saw an awe-inspiring vision of God.

Family links: Isaiah was the son of Amoz. He lived in Jerusalem. We are not told the name of Isaiah's wife. She is just called "the prophetess" in *Isaiah 8:3*.

Isaiah gave his children significant names. His first son was called Shear-Jashub meaning "a remnant will return." Isaiah's second son was called, Maher-Shalal-Hash-Baz, meaning, "quick to the plunder." "And the Lord said to me, 'Name him Maher-Shalal-Hash-Baz. Before the boy knows how to say "My father" or "My mother," the wealth of Damascus and the plunder of Samaria will be carried off by the king of Assyria'" *Isaiah 8:3,4*. This meant that the enemies of King Ahaz would be plundered.

New Testament link: *Isaiah 7:14* is quoted in *Matthew 1:23* as a prophecy about the virgin birth of Jesus.

Quote: "My eyes have seen the King, the Lord Almighty." *Isaiah 6:5*

Link to Jesus: Jesus fulfilled *Isaiah 42:1-4*. See *Matthew 12:18-21*.

Key verses: *Isaiah 52:13–53:12* is the most detailed Old Testament prophecy about the death of Jesus, the messiah and suffering servant.

More Information: The whole of the book of *Isaiah,* especially *Isaiah 1:1; 7:3; 8:1-4*

Isaiah and the kings of Judah

According to the opening verse of the book of Isaiah, the prophet gave his prophecies during the reigns of Uzziah, Jotham, Ahaz, and Hezekiah.

There were nine kings of Judah before this: Rehoboam, Abijam, Asa, Jehoshaphat, Jehoram, Ahaziah, Athaliah, Joash, and Amaziah.

After Isaiah's ministry there were seven further kings of Judah, before Jerusalem fell to the Babylonians in 586 BC: Manasseh, Amon, Josiah, Jehoahaz, Jehoiakim, Jehoiachin, and Zedekiah.

Jonah

Jonah

Meaning of name: Dove

Point of interest: Jonah was swallowed by a great fish. Jonah was the first Hebrew prophet to be sent into a Gentile (non-Jewish) country. He prophesied during the reign of King Jeroboam II of Israel.

Family links: Jonah's father was Amittai: *Jonah 1:1.* Jonah came from Gath Hepher, *2 Kings 14:25,* a Zebulunite town near to Nazareth.

New Testament link: Jesus mentioned Jonah. "A wicked and adulterous generation asks for a miraculous sign! But none will be given it except the sign of the prophet Jonah. For as Jonah was in the belly of a huge fish, so the Son of Man will be three days and three nights in the heart of the earth." *Matthew 12:39,40*

Quote: In chapter 2 of Jonah's prophecy, the prophet records his prayer from the belly of the huge fish: "In my distress I called to the Lord, and he answered me. From the depths of the grave I called for help, and you listened to my cry." *Jonah 2:2*

Link to Jesus: Jesus likened Jonah's experience in the belly of the fish to his own resurrection. Jesus told some of the Pharisees and teachers of the law that the sign of the prophet Jonah was the only miraculous sign they needed to see.

Key verse: From the seaport of Joppa Nineveh was 500 miles northeast across desert. Going to Tarshish meant traveling 2,000 miles west. "But Jonah ran away from the Lord and headed for Tarshish." *Jonah 1:3*

More Information: *2 Kings 14:25;* the whole of the book of *Jonah; Matthew 12:29-31; 16:4, 17*

Jeremiah

Jeremiah

Meaning of name: God is high

Point of interest: Jeremiah was the great prophet of Judah who prophesied, from about 625–585 BC, during the grim reigns of the last five kings of Judah: Josiah, Jehoahaz, Jehoiakim, Jehoiachin, and Zedekiah.

Family links: "The words of Jeremiah son of Hilkiah, one of the priests at Anathoth in the territory of Benjamin." *Jeremiah 1:1*

New Testament link: One of the most renowned prophecies made by Jeremiah concerns his description of a new covenant.

"'The time is coming,' declares the Lord,
'when I will make a new covenant with the house of Israel
and with the house of Judah.
It will not be like the covenant
I made with their forefathers
when I took them by the hand
to lead them out of Egypt,
because they broke my covenant,
though I was a husband to them,'
declares the Lord.
'This is the covenant that I will make
with the house of Israel
after that time,' declares the Lord.
'I will put my law in their minds
and write it on their hearts.
I will be their God,
and they will be my people.'"
Jeremiah 31:31-33
Compare this with *Hebrews 8:8-10; 10:16, 17.*

Quote: "Can the Ethiopian change his skin or the leopard its spots?" *Jeremiah 13:23*

Link to Jesus: Jeremiah speaks of "The Lord our Righteousness." *Jeremiah 23:6.* Paul explains how Jesus is our righteousness in *Romans 3:21, 22.*

Key verse: Jeremiah constantly called the Israelites to obey God. "Obey me, and I will be your God and you will be my people." *Jeremiah 7:23*

More Information: The whole of the book of *Jeremiah.*

Jeremiah: the prophet no one listened to

Jeremiah was given a thankless task by God. For 40 years Jeremiah warned the people who lived in Jerusalem that unless they turned back to God they would be captured and taken away by the Babylonians. Most of the time his preaching fell on deaf ears.

- Jeremiah was rejected: *Jeremiah 11:18-21.*
- Even Jeremiah's friends were fickle: *Jeremiah 12:2-6.*
- Jeremiah was plagued by false prophets. He confronted them face to face: *Jeremiah 14:13-16; 28:10-17.*
- Jeremiah was often threatened with violence and endured persecution: *Jeremiah 15:10-18.*

Jeremiah's prophecy comes true

Jeremiah not only warned the people that Jerusalem would be captured, he also predicted that the Israelites would return to Jerusalem 70 years later.

1. Jerusalem was captured

"Nebuzaradan commander of the imperial guard, who served the king of Babylon, came to Jerusalem. He set fire to the temple of the Lord, the royal palace and all the houses of Jerusalem. Every important building he burned down." *Jeremiah 52:12,13*

- Jeremiah predicted this in *Jeremiah 25:8-11*.
- The book of *Lamentations*, also written by Jeremiah, is a description of Jerusalem after it had been ransacked.

2. Israelites return to Jerusalem

70 years later Cyrus, king of Persia, allowed Israelites to return to Jerusalem. See *2 Chronicles 36:15-23*.

Deportation of Assyrian captives

- Jeremiah was put in the stocks: *Jeremiah 20:1,2*.
- On a number of occasions Jeremiah barely escaped with his life: *Jeremiah 26:8, 36:26*.
- Accused of treason, Jeremiah was imprisoned: *Jeremiah 32:2,3; 37:11-15*.
- Jeremiah had some of his prophecies burned by King Jehoiakim: *Jeremiah 36:22-25*.

- Jeremiah was lowered by ropes into a cistern and left to die: *Jeremiah 38:6*. If it had not been for the courage of Ebed-Melech, who alerted King Zedekiah to the evil behind this action, Jeremiah would have died. As it was, Ebed-Melech rescued him.
- Jeremiah was bound in chains: *Jeremiah 40:1*.

Esther

Esther

Point of interest: Esther saved the Jews from being massacred.

Family links: Esther was an orphan. She was brought up by her uncle, Mordecai.

New Testament link: Esther is not mentioned in the New Testament.

Quote: "Esther said, 'The adversary and enemy is this vile Haman.'" *Esther 7:6*

Link to Jesus: Mordecai has been seen as a type of Jesus for the following reasons:

- Mordecai adopted Esther: *Esther 2:7* Although we were orphans, and in the world without hope, Jesus received us into God's family: *John 1:12; Ephesians 2:8, 9, 12, 13.*

- As Mordecai was despised, *Esther 3:5,* so was Jesus, *Isaiah 53:3; John 15:25.*

- As Mordecai was tested, *Esther 4:1,* so was Jesus, *Matthew 4:1-11; Luke 22:42.*

- As Mordecai finally received a place of honor, *Esther 6:1-3; 8:7,8,* so did Jesus in his resurrection, *Ephesians 1:20-23; Hebrews 1:3.*

Key verse: "'For if you remain silent at this time, relief and deliverance for the Jews will arise from another place, but you and your father's family will perish. And who knows but that you have come to royal position for such a time as this.'" *Esther 4:14*

More Information: The whole book of Esther.

The beauty queen

When King Xerxes looked for a new wife a competition took place to find him "beautiful young virgins," *Esther 2:2.* Esther, "who was lovely in form and features," *Esther 2:7,* won the beauty competition and became the new queen.

Brave Esther

When Mordecai told Esther that the king's minister, Haman, plotted to kill all the Jews, Esther pleaded with Xerxes for the Jews, even though she risked her own life in doing this.

Daniel

Daniel

Meaning of name: "God is my judge"

Point of interest: Daniel was thrown into a lions' den, and spending a whole night with them, without being harmed.

Family links: Daniel came from an aristocratic Jerusalem family, but apart from that we know nothing about his family. When Jerusalem was captured by Nebuchadnezzar, Daniel, as a teenager, was exiled to Babylon, where he rose to prominence because of his ability to interpret dreams. Following the custom of the time he was given a Babylonian name, Belteshazzar, *Daniel 1:7*.

New Testament link: The allusion in *Hebrews 11:33* to lions, "who shut the mouths of lions," seems a clear reference to Daniel's experience recorded in *Daniel 6*.

Quote: "O king, live forever! My God sent his angel, and he shut the mouths of the lions. They have not hurt me, because I was found innocent in his sight." *Daniel 6:22*

Link to Jesus: Jesus is seen by Daniel:
- as the Ancient of Days, *Daniel 7:9*
- a son of man, *Daniel 7:13*
- the Prince of princes, *Daniel 8:25*
- the most holy, *Daniel 9:24,*
- the Anointed One, *Daniel 9:25*.

Key verse: "'In my visions ... one like a son of man ... was given authority, glory, and sovereign power; all peoples, nations and men of every language worshiped him. His dominion is an everlasting dominion that will not pass away, and his kingdom is one that will never be destroyed.'" *Daniel 7:13, 14*

More Information: The whole book of *Daniel; Matthew 24:15*

Ezekiel and the prophets of Judah

Not well received

Many of Ezekiel's prophecies were badly received.

> "And you, son of man, they will tie with ropes; you will be bound so that you cannot go out among the people."
> *Ezekiel 3:25*

Not followed

Even when the Jews did listen to Ezekiel they did not do what he told them to.

> "Indeed, to them you are nothing more than one who sings love songs with a beautiful voice and plays an instrument well, for they hear your words but do not put them into practice." *Ezekiel 33:32*

Ezekiel and salvation

Ezekiel gives many pictures and visions depicting what happens when God saves us. In chapter 16 Ezekiel says that:

- God makes us alive: *verse 6*
- God cleanses and washes us: *verse 9*
- God clothes us: *verses 8,11*
- God claims us for himself: *verse 8*
- God crowns us: *verse 12*.

Ezekiel

Meaning of name: God strengthens

Point of interest: Ezekiel comforted the Jews who were in exile in Babylon. Ezekiel had been exiled from Jerusalem and lived in Babylon with a community of Jews at Talabib on the River Chebar, *Ezekiel 1:1*. There he told the Jews that God would restore Jerusalem to them and they would be able to rebuild God's temple.

Family links: Ezekiel was the son of Buzi the priest. Ezekiel's wife died the day Nebuchadnezzar besieged Jerusalem, *Ezekiel 24:1,2, 15-17*. No mention is made of any children.

New Testament link: Ezekiel predicts a caring shepherd, calling him "my servant David," "'I will place over them one shepherd, my servant David, and he will tend them; he will tend them and be their shepherd.'" *Ezekiel 34: 23*. A favorite description of Jesus is recorded in John's Gospel, "'I am the good shepherd. The good shepherd lays down his life for the sheep.'" *John 10:11*

Quote: "You will know that I am the Lord." *Ezekiel 6:7*. This phrase comes more than 60 times in the book named after Ezekiel.

Link to Jesus:

- *Ezekiel 17: 22-24*, depicts the Messiah as a tender twig that becomes a stately cedar on a high mountain. Jesus is also called the Branch in *Isaiah 11:1; Jeremiah 24:5; 33:15;* and *Zechariah 3:8; 6:12*.

- The Messiah is the King who has the right to rule, *Ezekiel 21:26,27*, and he is the true Shepherd who will deliver and feed his flock, *Ezekiel 34:11-31*.

Key verse: "The hand of the Lord was upon me, and he brought me out by the Spirit of the Lord and set me in the middle of a valley; it was full of bones." *Ezekiel 37:1*

More Information: The whole book of *Ezekiel*

35

The prophets of Judah

Five prophets, who do not have books in the Bible named after them, nevertheless prophesied to the people of Judah:

- Shemaiah
- Hanani
- Huldah.
- Azariah
- Jahaziel

Seven prophets, who do have books in the Bible recording their prophecies, spoke to the people of Judah:

- Joel
- Micah
- Habakkuk
- Ezekiel.
- Isaiah
- Zephaniah
- Jeremiah

Ezra

Ezra

Meaning of name: The Lord helps

Point of interest: Ezra led a second group of Israelite exiles from Babylon back to Jerusalem. In this way Ezra shows how God fulfilled his promise to return his people to Jerusalem after their 70 years of exile.

New Testament link: Ezra shows how God kept his promise to keep David's descendants alive. Zerubbabel, a leader of a group who returned from exile *(Ezra 3–5)* is part of the messianic line as he was the grandson of Jeconiah. See *1 Chronicles 3:17-19* and *Matthew 1:12,13*.

Quote: "'O my God, I am too ashamed and disgraced to lift up my face to you, my God, because our sins are higher than our heads and our guilt has reached to the heavens." *Ezra 9:7*

Link to Jesus: The book of Ezra as a whole typifies Jesus' work of forgiveness and restoration.

Key verse: "For Ezra had devoted himself to the study and observance of the Law of the Lord, and to teaching its decrees and laws in Israel." *Ezra 7:10*

More Information: The whole book of *Ezra; Nehemiah 8:1-9; 12:36*

Godly Ezra

Ezra was a godly man with:
• a strong trust in the Lord:
  Ezra 9:6-15
• moral integrity:
  Ezra 10:9-17
• an outrage about people sinning against God:
  Ezra 9:3,4.

Nehemiah

Nehemiah

Meaning of name: The Lord comforts

Point of interest: Nehemiaf rebuilt the walls of Jerusalem.

Family links: All we are told about Nehemiah comes from the book named after him. He was the son of Hacaliah and had a brother called Hanani, *Nehemiah 1:1, 2; 7:2.* Nehemiah held the privileged position of being cupbearer to the Persian king, Artaxerxes I, 465–424 BC, *Nehemiah 1:11.*

Quote: "But the early governors – those preceding me – placed a heavy burden on the people and took forty shekels of silver from them in addition to food and wine. Their assistants also lorded it over the people. But out of reverence for God I did not act like that. Instead, I devoted myself to the work on this wall." *Nehemiah 5:15,16*

Link to Jesus: Like Ezra, Nehemiah portrays Jesus in his ministry of reconciliation:

- Nehemiah, like Jesus, gave up a high position in order to identify with the plight of his people.
- Nehemiah, like Jesus, came with a specific mission and fulfilled it.
- Nehemiah, like Jesus, lived a life of dependance on God.

Key verse: "So the wall was completed on the twenty-fifth of Elul [22 October 445 BC], in fifty-two days." *Nehemiah 6:15*

More Information: The whole book of *Nehemiah*

Nehemiah and prayer

- Nehemiah began his work in prayer: *Nehemiah 1:4.*
- Nehemiah continued his work in prayer: *Nehemiah 4:9.*
- Nehemiah did not stop praying when he had finished his work: *Nehemiah 13:31.*

Joseph

Joseph

Meaning of name: May (God) add

Family links: Joseph, a carpenter, was a descendant of king David: see *Matthew 1:20*. His wife was Mary.

Link with Jesus:

- Joseph acted as a father towards Jesus.
- Joseph took Jesus to Jerusalem for the purification, *Luke 2:2*.
- Joseph took the toddler Jesus and Mary to Egypt, to escape King Herod's murderous intentions.
- Joseph took Jesus and Mary from Egypt to Nazareth and settled there, *Matthew 2:19-23*.
- Joseph took Jesus to Jerusalem for the Passover, *Luke 2:41*.

- It seems probable that at least by the time Jesus was twelve years old he knew that Joseph was not his father. "'Why were you searching for me?' he [Jesus] asked. 'Didn't you know I had to be in my Father's house?'" *Luke 2:49*

Key verse: "'Joseph son of David, do not be afraid to take Mary home as your wife, because what is conceived in her is from the Holy Spirit." *Matthew 1:20*

More Information: *Matthew 1:20-25; 2:13-23; Luke 1:27–2:52*

Joseph obeys

Little is known about Jesus' foster father Joseph. But his utter obedience to God is clear from the way he obeyed what God told him to do in his dreams.

- "The Lord appeared to him [Joseph] in a dream and said, 'Joseph … take Mary home as your wife.'" *Matthew 1:20*

- "An angel of the Lord appeared to Joseph in a dream. 'Get up,' he said, 'take the child and his mother and escape to Egypt.' … So he got up, took the child and his mother during the night and left for Egypt." *Matthew 2:13,14*.

- "An angel of the Lord appeared in a dream to Joseph in Egypt and said, 'Get up, take the child and his mother and go to the land of Israel.'" *Matthew 2:19,20*

What happened to Joseph?

The last time we hear about Joseph being alive was when Jesus visited the temple as a twelve-year-old. Joseph is not mentioned during Jesus' ministry.

Mary

Mary

Meaning of name: "Mary" is a form of "Miriam" meaning "strong"

Point of interest: Mary was the mother of Jesus.

Family links: Mary was living in Nazareth, a town in Galilee, engaged to Joseph, when an angel told Mary that, although she was still a virgin, she would be the mother of Jesus. Mary visited her relative Elizabeth who later gave birth to John the Baptist.

Old Testament link: Mary knew that the birth of Jesus was in fulfillment of the prophecy of *Isaiah 7:14*, which stated that a virgin would give birth to a son. See *Matthew 1:22,23*.

Quote: "'I am the Lord's servant,' Mary answered. 'May it be to me as you have said.'" *Luke 1:38*

Link with Jesus: Mary was not only the mother of Jesus, but was also present at different points in Jesus' ministry, such as the turning of water into wine at Cana, *John 2:1-22*. Mary also watched Jesus being crucified, and was with Jesus' apostles after Jesus' resurrection. "They all joined together constantly in prayer, along with the women and Mary the mother of Jesus, and with his brothers." *Acts 1:14*

Key verse: "His mother [Mary] said to the servants, 'Do whatever he [Jesus] tells you.'" *Luke 2:5*

More Information: *Matthew 1–2; Mark 3:31-35; Luke 1–2; 11:27,28; John 2:1-22; 19:25-27; Acts 1:14*

Mary's faith

Mary expressed her faith when on her visit to Elizabeth, she said a song of praise, which we now call the Magnificat.

> "My soul glorifies the Lord
>   and my spirit rejoices in God
>   my savior,
> for he has been mindful
>   of the humble state of his
>   servant."
> *Luke 1:46-48*

The life of Jesus

Jesus

Meaning of name: The Lord is salvation

Point of interest: Jesus is the Savior of the world.

Family links: Jesus' conception was miraculous. Mary was still a virgin when Jesus was conceived. The angel told the virgin Mary, "You will be with child and give birth to a son, and you are to give him the name Jesus." *Luke 1:31*

Matthew traces Jesus' family tree through Joseph back to Abraham. "A record of the genealogy of Jesus Christ the son of David, the son of Abraham." *Matthew 1:1*

Luke traces Jesus' family tree back to Adam: *Luke 3:23-38.*

Old Testament link: "'Do not think that I have come to abolish the Law or the Prophets; I have not come to abolish them but to fulfill them.'" *Matthew 5:17*

Quote: Jesus' crucifixion was planned by God and did not take Jesus by surprise. In the same way Jesus' resurrection should not have taken the disciples by surprise. "And he [Jesus] said, 'The Son of Man must suffer many things and be rejected by the elders, chief priests and teachers of the law, and he must be killed and on the third day be raised to life.'" *Luke 9:21, 22*

Key verse: Jesus tells us who God is like. "In the past God spoke to our forefathers through the prophets at many times and in various ways, but in these last days he has spoken to us by his Son, whom he appointed heir of all things, and through whom he made the universe. The Son is the radiance of God's glory and the exact representation of his being, sustaining all things by his powerful word." *Hebrews 1:1-3*

More Information: The whole of *Matthew, Mark, Luke,* and *John*

Events in Jesus' life

Jesus' childhood

Event	Place	Date	Reference in the Gospels
Birth of Jesus	Bethlehem	c. 6/5 BC	*Matthew 1:18-25; Luke 2:1-7*
Visit by shepherds	Bethlehem		*Luke 2:8-20*
Presentation in the temple	Jerusalem		*Luke 2:21-40*
Visit by the Magi	Bethlehem		*Matthew 2:1-12*
Escape to Egypt	Nile Delta		*Matthew 2:13-18*
Return to Nazareth	Lower Galilee		*Matthew 2:19-23*
Visit to temple	Jerusalem	c. AD 7/8	*Luke 2:41-52*

None of the four Gospels give any details about Jesus' life from the time that he went to the temple, aged twelve years old, to when Jesus arrived at the River Jordan and was baptized by John the Baptist.

All we have is the following two-verse summary by Luke.

"Then he [Jesus] went down to Nazareth with them [Mary and Joseph] and was obedient to them. But his mother treasured all these things in her heart. And Jesus grew in wisdom and stature, and in favor with God and men." *Luke 2:51,52*

You would have thought that the one place where Jesus would be welcome was the place where he grew up. Yes and no. Yes, "All spoke well of him." *Luke 4:22*

No, "They got up, drove him [Jesus] out of the town, and took him to the brow of the hill ... in order to throw him down the cliff. But he walked right through the crowd and went on his way." *Luke 4:29,30*

First year of Jesus' public ministry

Event	Place	Date	Reference in the Gospels
Jesus is baptized	River Jordan	c. AD 26	*Matthew 3:13-17*
Jesus is tempted by Satan	Desert		*Matthew 4:1-11*
Jesus' first miracle	Cana		*John 2:1-11*
Jesus and Nicodemus	Jerusalem		*John 3:1-21*
Jesus and the Samaritan woman	Samaria	c. AD 27	*John 4:5-42*
Jesus heals the nobleman's son	Cana		*John 4:46-54*
People try to kill Jesus	Nazareth		*Luke 4:16-31*

Events in Jesus' life

Jesus' year of popularity

Event	Place	Date	Reference in the Gospels
Four fishermen follow Jesus	Capernaum	AD 28	*Matthew 3:13-17*
Jesus preaches in Galilee			*Matthew 4:23-25*
Jesus chooses his twelve disciples			*Mark 3:13-19*
Jesus preaches the Sermon on the Mount			*Matthew 5:1–7:29*

The most famous part of the Sermon on the Mount is the Beatitudes:

"Blessed are the poor in spirit, for theirs is the kingdom of heaven.
Blessed are those who mourn, for they will be comforted.
Blessed are the meek, for they will inherit the earth.
Blessed are those who hunger and thirst for righteousness, for they will be filled.
Blessed are the merciful, for they will be shown mercy.
Blessed are the pure in heart, for they will see God.
Blessed are the peacemakers, for they will be called sons of God.
Blessed are those who are persecuted because of righteousness, for theirs is the kingdom of heaven.
Blessed are you when people insult you, persecute you and falsely say all kinds of evil against you because of me.
Rejoice and be glad, because great is your reward in heaven, for in the same way they persecuted the prophets who were before you."
Matthew 5:1-12

Jesus' year of opposition

Event	Place	Date	Reference in the Gospels
John the Baptist beheaded	Machaerus	AD 29	*Matthew 14:1-12*
Peter says Jesus is the Son of God	Caesarea Philippi		*Matthew 16:21-26*
Jesus is transfigured			*Matthew 17:1-13*
Jesus brings Lazarus back to life	Bethany		*John 11:1-44*
Jesus sets off for Jerusalem		AD 30	*Luke 17:11*

Jesus' last week

Event	Place	Day	Reference in the Gospels
Palm Sunday	Jerusalem	Sunday	*Matthew 21:1-11*
Jesus curses the fig-tree		Monday	*Matthew 21:18,19*
Jesus cleanses the temple		Monday	*Matthew 21:18,19*
Jesus' authority challenged		Tuesday	*Matthew 21:23-27*
Jesus teaches in the temple		Tuesday	*Matthew 21:28–23:39*
Jesus is anointed	Bethany	Tuesday	*Matthew 26:6-13*
Jesus is plotted against	Jerusalem	Wednesday	*Matthew 26:17-29*
The Last Supper		Thursday	*Matthew 26:17-29*
Jesus teaches his disciples		Thursday	*John 14:1–16:33*
Jesus in the Garden of Gethsemane		Thursday	*Matthew 26:36-46*
Jesus' arrest and trials		Thurs/Fri	*Matthew 26:47–27:26*
Jesus is crucified		Friday	*Matthew 27:27-56*
Jesus is buried	Joseph's tomb	Friday	*Matthew 27:57-66*

43

In his life

"In his life Christ is an example,
showing us how to live;
In his death he is a sacrifice,
satisfying for our sins;

In his resurrection, a conqueror;
In his ascension, a king;
In his intercession, a high
priest." *Martin Luther*

Jesus' resurrection

Event	Place	Day	Reference in the Gospels
The empty tomb	Jerusalem	Sunday	*Matthew 28:1-10*
Mary Magdalene sees the risen Jesus	Jerusalem	Sunday	*Mark 16:9-11*
Jesus appears to the two going to	Emmaus	Sunday	*Mark 16:12,13*
Jesus appears to ten disciples	Jerusalem	Sunday	*John 20:19-25*
Jesus appears to eleven disciples	Jerusalem	1wk later	*John 20:26-31*
Jesus talks to some of his disciples	Sea of Galilee	1 wk later	*John 21:1-25*
Jesus ascends to his Father in heaven	Mount of Olives	40 days later	*Luke 24:44-53*

Elizabeth and Zechariah

Elizabeth

Meaning of name: God is my oath

Point of interest: Elizabeth was the mother of John the Baptist. This was a miraculous conception as Elizabeth was barren and "well on in years." See *Luke 1:7*.

Family links: Wife of Zechariah, who was also descended from the high priest Aaron.

Quote: When Mary visited Elizabeth, Elizabeth greeted Mary with the words: "Blessed are you among women, and blessed is the child you shall bear!" *Luke 1:42*

Link with Jesus: Elizabeth's son baptized Jesus.

Key verse: "When Elizabeth heard Mary's greeting, the baby leaped in her womb, and Elizabeth was filled with the Holy Spirit." *Luke 1:41*

More Information: *Luke 1*

Zechariah

Meaning of name: The Lord remembers

Point of interest: Zechariah was the father of John the Baptist.

Family links: Zechariah was a godly priest who belonged to the priestly division of Abijah.

Old Testament link: David had separated the priests into different divisions "for their appointed order of ministering." *1 Chronicles 24:3* "The eighth [lot fell] to Abijah." *1 Chronicles 24:10*

Quote: When an angel told Zechariah that his wife Elizabeth would have a son, Zechariah was incredulous. So Zechariah was unable to speak until his baby was born and named John.

Link with Jesus: Zechariah's son baptized Jesus.

Key verse: "Then they made signs to his father, to find out what he would like to name the child. He asked for a writing tablet, and to everyone's astonishment he wrote, 'His name is John.'" *Luke 1:63*

More Information: *Luke 1*

Simeon and Anna

Two people in the temple

When Joseph and Mary took the baby Jesus to the temple in Jerusalem, just five miles from Bethlehem, in order to present him to the Lord, they met two godly people.

Simeon

Meaning of name: He hears

Point of interest: Simeon was given special insight by God's Spirit to recognize Jesus as the Christ.

Quote: The words Simeon said of Jesus are sometimes called the *Nunc Dimittis*, after the first words of the Latin Vulgate translation: "[You] now dismiss."

Link with Jesus: Simeon took him [Jesus] in his arms and praised God, saying: "Sovereign Lord, as you have promised, you now dismiss your servant in peace." *Luke 2:29*

More Information: *Luke 2:25-35*

Anna

Meaning of name: Grace

Point of interest: Anna greeted the baby Jesus in the temple, whom she recognized as the Messiah.

Family links: Daughter of Phanuel, of the tribe of Asher.

Old Testament link: Anna was a prophetess, *Luke 2:36*. Prophetesses in the Old Testament include Miriam, *Exodus 15:20;* Deborah, *Judges 4:4*, and Huldah, *2 Kings 22:14.*

Link with Jesus: "Coming up to them [Joseph, Mary, and the baby Jesus] at that very moment, she gave thanks to God and spoke about the child to all who were looking forward to the redemption of Jerusalem." *Luke 2:38*

Key verse: Anna was very old, either 84 years old, or she had been a widow for 84 years, which would make her over 100 years old. "She never left the temple but worshiped night and day, fasting and praying." *Luke 2:37*

More Information: *Luke 2:36-38*

Augustus, Tiberius, and Herod

Augustus

Meaning of name: "August"
Point of interest: When he became the first Roman Emperor he took the name Octavian, ruling from 31 BC to AD 14. The census which brought Joseph and Mary to Bethlehem for Jesus' birth was ordered by Augustus.
Family links: He was the nephew and successor of Julius Caesar.
More Information: See *Luke 2:1*

Tiberius

Meaning of name: "Son of Tiber"
Point of interest: Also known as Claudius Caesar Augustus. He was Roman Emperor from AD 14 to AD 37, that is during most of Jesus' lifetime.
Key verse: "In the fifteenth year of the reign of Tiberius Caesar ... " *Luke 3:1*

Herod

Meaning of name: [Herod, known as Herod the Great] Heroic
Point of interest: Herod ordered the massacre of all the male babies under the age of two in Bethlehem.
Family links: By murdering his rivals Herod became king of Judea in 37 BC, and ruled until 4 BC. Herod murdered many of his sons, fearing their plots against him.
Quote: To the Magi, Herod said, "Go and make a careful search for the child. As soon as you find him, report to me, so that I too may go and worship him." *Matthew 2:8*

Link with Jesus: Joseph took Mary and Jesus to Egypt after he had been warned in a dream that Herod was "going to search for the child to kill him." *Matthew 2:13*
Key verse: "After Jesus was born in Bethlehem in Judea, during the time of King Herod ... " *Matthew 2:1*. As Herod died in 4 BC, we know that Jesus must have been born before 4 BC, rather than in 0 AD.
More Information: *Matthew 2; Luke 1:5*

John the Baptist

John

Meaning of name: The Lord is gracious

Point of interest: John baptized Jesus.

Family links: John's Father, Zechariah, was a priest. As John's mother, Elizabeth, was related to Mary the mother of Jesus, John was related to Jesus.

Old Testament link: John looked like an Old Testament prophet, with his camels' hair clothes and leather belt. He lived in the desert eating wild honey and locusts.

Luke said that John fulfilled Isaiah's prophecy:

"A voice of one calling in the desert, 'Prepare the way for the Lord, make straight paths for him ...

And all mankind will see God's salvation.'" *Luke 3:4-6*

Quote: John was outspoken in his condemnation of the Pharisees and Sadducees. "He said to them: 'You brood of vipers! Who warned you to flee from the coming wrath? Produce fruit in keeping with repentance. And do not think you can say to yourselves, "We have Abraham as our father."' *Matthew 3:7-9*

Link with Jesus: Speaking about John the Baptist, Jesus said, "'I tell you the truth: Among those born of women there has not risen anyone greater than John the Baptist ... " *Matthew 11:11*

Key verse: John the Baptist told Herod the tetrach off for marrying his brother Philip's wife while Philip was still alive. This led to John being beheaded. "'It is not lawful for you to have her.'" *Matthew 14:4*

More Information: *Matthew 3; 11:1-19; 14:1-12; Mark 1:1-8; Luke 1; John 1:1-34*

Peter

Meaning of name: Rock

Point of interest: Peter said that Jesus was the Christ. "'Who do you say I am?' Simon Peter answered, 'You are the Christ, the Son of the living God.'" *Matthew 16:16*

Family links: Andrew was Peter's brother.

Old Testament link: On the Day of Pentecost, when Peter preached the first Christian sermon, he included the following quotation from *Joel 2:28:* "'In the last days, God says, I will pour out my Spirit on all people.'" *Acts 2:17*

Quote: Peter denied knowing Jesus three times. "Then he [Peter] began to call down curses on himself and he swore to them, 'I don't know the man!'" *Matthew 26:74*

Link with Jesus: In the list of Jesus' twelve apostles Peter always comes at the top of the list as he was their outspoken leader.

Key verse: Although Peter had been tempestuous as a young follower of Jesus, in his old age he encouraged others with these words: "Humble yourselves, therefore, under God's mighty hand, that he may lift you up in due course." *1 Peter 5:6*

More Information: *Acts 1–12;* the whole of *1 Peter* and *2 Peter*. Peter is often mentioned in the four Gospels.

Peter and the New Testament

Traditionally it is thought that much of Mark's Gospel was derived from Peter and may have been a summary of his preaching.

The two letters *1 Peter* and *2 Peter* were written by Peter.

Peter's death

According to tradition Peter was crucified upside-down in Rome in the AD 60s, during the reign of Nero.

Andrew

Andrew

Meaning of name: Manly

Point of interest: Andrew introduced Peter to Jesus.

Family links: Andrew, with his brother Peter, and with James and John, ran a small fishing partnership on Lake Galilee.

Quote: Andrew brought a boy, who had his own packed lunch, to Jesus, which Jesus miraculously used to feed more than 5,000 people. "Andrew, Simon Peter's brother, spoke up, 'Here is a boy with five small barley loaves and two small fish, but how far will they go among so many?'" *John 6:8, 9*

Link with Jesus: Andrew became one of Jesus' first disciples.

Key verse: "Andrew, Simon Peter's brother, was one of the two who heard what John had said and who had followed Jesus. The first thing Andrew did was to find his brother Simon and tell him, 'We have found the Messiah' (that is, the Christ). And he brought him to Jesus." *John 1:40-42*

More Information: *Matthew 4:18-20; Mark 1:16-18; John 1:35-42; 6:8,9*

Loaves and fish: mosaic at Tabgha, on the shores of Lake Galilee.

James

James

Meaning of name: "James" is a form of "Jacob" which means "supplanter"

Point of interest: James was one of Jesus' disciples.

Family links: James' brother was John, another of Jesus' disciples. The two brothers, with their father, Zebedee, ran a small family business as fishermen. James and John were given the nicknames of "Sons of Thunder," presumably because they had stormy natures. "Jesus … appointed twelve … apostles … James son of Zebedee and his brother John (to them he gave the name Boanerges, which means Sons of Thunder)." *Mark 3:13,14,17*

Old Testament link: When Jesus was setting out for Jerusalem he sent messengers ahead of him to a Samaritan village to get things ready for him. However, this village did not welcome Jesus. The Sons of Thunder then asked Jesus, "'Lord, do you want us to call fire down from heaven to destroy them?'" *Luke 9:54.* This is an allusion to the prophet Elijah. "Elijah answered the captain, 'If I am a man of God, may fire come down from heaven and consume you and your fifty men!' Then the fire fell from heaven and consumed the captain and his men." *2 Kings 1:9*

Link with Jesus: James was called by Jesus to be one of his special followers. "When he [Jesus] had gone a little farther, he saw James son of Zebedee and his brother John in a boat, preparing their nets. Without delay he called them, and they left their father Zebedee in the boat with the hired men and followed him." *Mark 1:9-20*

Key verse: With Peter and his brother John, James became one of Jesus' inner circle of three friends and experienced special moments with Jesus, such as the transfiguration of Jesus. "After six days Jesus took with him Peter, James and John the brother of James, and led them up a high mountain by themselves." *Matthew 17:1*

More Information: *Matthew 4:21,22; 10:2; 17:1-13; 26:37; Mark 5:37; 10:35-45; Luke 9:51-56; Acts 12:2*

James' death

James was beheaded by Herod Agrippa I about ten years after Jesus' death. See *Acts 12:2*.

John

John

Meaning of name: The Lord is gracious

Point of interest: John was "the disciple whom Jesus loved." In John's Gospel, the author, John, never mentions himself by name, but instead uses the expression, "the disciple whom Jesus loved." See *John 13:23; 19:26; 21:7.*

Family links: John's brother was James, also one of Jesus' disciples, and their father was Zebedee.

Old Testament link: John, the writer of the fourth Gospel, was a Jew and clearly very familiar with the Old Testament. He begins his Gospel with the words, "In the beginning was the Word, and the Word was with God, and the Word was God," an echo of *Genesis 1:1:* "In the beginning God created the heavens and the earth."

Quote: "Lord, who is going to betray you?" *John 21:20*

Link with Jesus: Jesus must have completely trusted John as he entrusted his mother into his care. "Near the cross of Jesus stood his mother … When Jesus saw his mother there, and the disciple whom he loved standing nearby, he said to his mother, 'Dear woman, here is your son,' and to the disciple, 'Here is your mother.' From that time on, this disciple took her into his home." *John 19:25-27*

Key verse: John not only wrote the fourth Gospel, but also three New Testament letters, 1, 2, and 3 John, as well as the book of Revelation. John states why he wrote his Gospel: "Jesus did many other miraculous signs in the presence of his disciples, which are not recorded in this book. But these are written that you may believe that Jesus is the Christ, the Son of God, and that by believing you may have life in his name." *John 20:30,31*

More Information: *Matthew 4:21,22; 20:20-23; John 13:23-25; 19:25-27; Acts 1:13; 3–4; Galatians 2:9; 1, 2, and 3 John, Revelation 1:1*

The other apostles and Matthias

Bartholomew

Meaning of name: Son of Talmai

Link with Jesus: We know nothing about Bartholomew who is only mentioned in the New Testament in the list of all Jesus' apostles. See *Matthew 10:3*

James

Meaning of name: "James" is a form of "Jacob" which means "supplanter"

Family links: Two of Jesus' twelve apostles were called James. This James, who was not the brother of John, is identified as the son of Alphaeus, but nothing more is known about him. See *Matthew 10:3; Acts 1:13*

Judas

Meaning of name: Praise

This Judas is to be identified as the same person who is called Thaddaeus. To distinguish him from the Judas who betrayed Jesus, this Judas is called, "Judas, not Iscariot."See *Luke 6:16; Acts 1:13*

Judas Iscariot

Meaning of name: Judas means "praise" Iscariot means "a man of Keriot," a town twelve miles from Hebron

Family links: Judas was the son of a man called Simon.

Link with Jesus: Judas, the treasurer for the twelve apostles, betrayed Jesus for 30 silver pieces. When John asked Jesus at the Last Supper which of the twelve apostles would betray him, Jesus replied: "It is the one to whom I will give this piece of bread when I have dipped it in the dish." *John 13:26.* Jesus then gave this piece of bread to Judas. "As soon as Judas took the bread, Satan entered into him." *John 13:27.* John adds, "As soon as Judas had taken the bread, he went out. And it was night." *John 13:30*

Judas betrayed Jesus with a kiss, a mark of friendship, in the Garden of Gethsemane so Jesus could be identified in the dark and arrested. Later, when Judas realized the wrong he had done, in a fit of remorse, he returned the 30 silver pieces to the priests and then committed suicide by hanging himself. See *Matthew 26:1–27:10; Acts 1:15-26*

Matthew

Meaning of name: Gift of the Lord

Link with Jesus: Matthew, who was also known as Levi, was a tax-collector when Jesus called him to follow him. Matthew then held a party in his home which Jesus went to. "While Jesus was having dinner at Levi's house, many tax collectors and 'sinners' were eating with him and his disciples, for there were many who followed him. When the teachers of the law who were Pharisees saw him eating with 'sinners' and tax collectors, they asked his disciples: 'Why does he eat with tax collectors and sinners?'" *Mark 2:15, 16*

This indicates that tax collectors were greatly despised. Also, to the ordinary Jew, they were regarded as traitors, working for their occupying power, the Romans. Jesus gave this reply to the question the Pharisees asked: "'It is not the healthy who need a doctor, but the sick. I have not come to call the righteous, but sinners.'" *Mark 2:17*

Nathanael

Meaning of name: God has given

Link with Jesus: He is mentioned only in John's Gospel and is most likely to be identified as the Bartholomew who is mentioned in the other Gospels. Nathanael first heard about Jesus from Philip. "When Jesus saw Nathanael approaching, he said of him, 'Here is a true Israelite, in whom there is nothing false.'" *John 1:47*

Philip

Meaning of name: Lover of horses

Link with Jesus: Like Andrew and Peter, Philip was a fisherman from Bethsaida. He brought Bartholomew (Nathanael) to Jesus. In answer to Philip's question about the Father, Jesus said, "'Anyone who has seen me has seen the Father.'" *John 14:9*

Simon

Meaning of name: Hearing

Link with Jesus: This Simon, who was a different person from Simon Peter, was known as Simon the Zealot, because he was most probably a member of a revolutionary group who wanted to drive the Romans from Israel. See *Matthew 10:4*

53

Thomas

Meaning of name: Twin. Thomas' Greek name was Didymus

Link with Jesus: Thomas is forever labeled as "doubting" Thomas because he did not initially believe that Jesus rose from the dead. But when he did see the risen Lord Jesus he said to him, "'My Lord and my God!'" *John 20:28*

Matthias

Meaning of name: God's gift

Link with Jesus: Matthias replaced Judas as an apostle. See *Acts 1:23,26*

Nicodemus

Nicodemus meets Jesus

Jesus' conversation with Nicodemus and his following words include the most famous words from the Bible:

"Just as Moses lifted up the snake in the desert, so the Son of Man must be lifted up, that everyone who believes in him may have eternal life."
John 3:15

"For God so loved the world that he gave his one and only Son, that whoever believes in him may have eternal life."
John 3:16

Nicodemus stands up for Jesus

Jesus was not exactly the most popular man in town with the Jewish hierarchy. The chief priests and Pharisees were furious with the temple guards for not arresting Jesus and scornfully asked the guards, "Has any of the rulers or the Pharisees believed in him?"
John 7:48

Nicodemus bravely leapt to Jesus' defense, and asked, "Does our law condemn a man without first hearing him to find out what he is doing?"
John 7:51

Nicodemus helps to bury Jesus

The last cameo John's Gospel gives us of Nicodemus is when Nicodemus brought 75 pounds of "a mixture of myrrh and aloes" to help Joseph of Arimathea bury Jesus.
John 19:39

Caiaphas

Caiaphas

Meaning of name: Depression

Point of interest: Caiaphas masterminded Jesus' arrest and condemnation.

Family links: Caiaphas was son-in-law of Annas who had been high priest from AD 6 to 13.

Old Testament link: The work of the Old Testament high priesthood is found in *Deuteronomy 33:8-10*. Caiaphas was an important member of the Jewish priesthood and was high priest in Jerusalem from AD 18 to 36.

Quote: Caiaphas advised the Jewish authorities that one man, Jesus, should die for all the people. "Then … Caiaphas, who was high priest that year, spoke up, … 'You do not realize that it is better for you that one man die for the people than that the whole nation perish.' He did not say this on his own, but as high priest that year he prophesied that Jesus would die for the Jewish nation, and not only for that nation but also for the scattered children of God, to bring them together and make them one." *John 11:51, 52*

Link with Jesus: Caiaphas presided over the illegal trial of Jesus when he was hauled up in front of the Sanhedrin. Caiaphas pronounced that Jesus was guilty of blasphemy.

Key verse: "Again the high priest asked him [Jesus], 'Are you the Christ, the Son of the Blessed One?' 'I am,' said Jesus." *Mark 14:61, 62*

More Information: *Matthew 26:3-5, 57-68; Mark 14:53-55; Luke 3:2; John 11:49-51; 18:12-14, 19-24; Acts 5:27*

Caiaphas and the first Christians

Caiaphas persecuted the early Christians:

"Having brought the apostles, they made them appear before the Sanhedrin to be questioned by the high priest. 'We gave you strict orders not to teach in this name,' he said. 'Yet you have filled Jerusalem with your teaching and are determined to make us guilty of this man's blood.' Peter and the other apostles replied: 'We must obey God rather than men!'"
Acts 5:27-29

Pilate

Pilate

Meaning of name: Javelin carrier

Point of interest: Pilate handed Jesus over to the Jews so that he would be crucified.

Pilate's position: Pilate was commander-in-chief of the Roman soldiers in Judea. Although the Jews hated the Romans they had to bring Jesus before Pilate as he could order the death sentence, which the Jews were not allowed to do.

Quote: Pilate had the following notice, written in Aramaic, Latin and Greek, put on Jesus' cross: "JESUS OF NAZARETH, THE KING OF THE JEWS." The chief priests protested to Pilate, "'Do not write "The King of the Jews," but that this man claimed to be king of the Jews.'" *John 19: 21*

To this, Pilate made his famous reply: "'What I have written, I have written.'" *John 19:22*

Link with Jesus: Pilate found Jesus "not guilty" of the false charges the Jews accused him of. "Once more Pilate came out and said to the Jews, 'Look, I am bringing him out to you to let you know that I find no basis for a charge against him.'" *John 19:4*

Key verse: "Finally Pilate handed him [Jesus] over to them to be crucified." *John 19:16*

More Information: *Matthew 27:11-26; Mark 15:1-15; Luke 22:66–23:25; John 18:28–19:22*

Pilate's wife

"While Pilate was sitting on the judge's seat, his wife sent him this message: 'Don't have anything to do with that innocent man, for I have suffered a great deal today in a dream because of him.'" *Matthew 27:19*

Stephen

Stephen

Meaning of name: Crown

Point of interest: Stephen was the first Christian martyr.

Family links: We know nothing about Stephen's family, but he was chosen to be one of the first seven deacons to be appointed who had to be full of the Spirit and wisdom. Stephen is described as being "a man full of faith and of the Holy Spirit." *Acts 6:5*

Old Testament link: When Stephen was brought before the Sanhedrin on trumped up charges of blasphemy against Moses and against God, he gave a lengthy defense in which he outlined the Old Testament account of the history of the Jews from the time of Abraham to Jesus' crucifixion.

Quote: "'Look,' he [Stephen] said, 'I see heaven open and the Son of Man standing at the right hand of God.'" *Acts 7:56*

Link with Jesus: As Stephen was being stoned to death he prayed a prayer which echoed some words spoken by Jesus as he was being crucified: "Stephen prayed, 'Lord Jesus, receive my spirit.' Then he fell on his knees and cried out, 'Lord, do not hold this sin against them.' When he had said this, he fell asleep." *Acts 7:59, 60*

Key verse: "All who were sitting in the Sanhedrin looked intently at Stephen, and they saw that his face was like the face of an angel." *Acts 6:15*

More Information: *Acts 6:1–8:2*

Stephen and Paul

It is left to our imaginations to work out how influential Stephen's martyrdom was. However, it clearly had a great effect on one man: "the witnesses laid their clothes at the feet of a young man named Saul … And Saul was there, giving approval to his death." *Acts 7:58; 8:1*

The stoning of Stephen, by Rembrant (1625) Musée des Beaux-Arts, Lyons

Cornelius

Cornelius

Meaning of name: Of a horn

Point of interest: Cornelius was one of the famous conversion stories in the Acts of the Apostles.

Family links: We know nothing of Cornelius' family, but we do know some facts about him:

- He was a Roman centurion in the Italian Regiment, living in Caesarea.
- He was respected by the Jews at Caesarea.
- He was well known for being generous to the poor.
- He and all his family prayed to God regularly.

Quote: "Cornelius answered: 'Four days ago I was in my house praying at this hour, at three in the afternoon. Suddenly a man in shining clothes stood before me and said, "Cornelius, God has heard your prayer and remembered your gifts to the poor.'"" *Acts 10:30, 31*

Link with Jesus: Peter went to Cornelius' home and preached the gospel to him and his family, saying, "You know the message God sent to the people of Israel, telling the good news of peace through Jesus Christ, who is Lord of all.'" *Acts 10:36* Whenever Peter preached he preached about Jesus.

Key verse: Cornelius, even though he was a high-ranking Roman soldier, showed his humility when Peter came into his home. "As Peter entered the house, Cornelius met him and fell at his feet in reverence." *Acts 10:25*

More Information: *Acts 10*

Jews and Christians

Many practicing Jews who became followers of Jesus found it hard to believe that Jesus' message applied to non-Jews as well.

> "The circumcised believers who had come with Peter were astonished that the gift of the Holy Spirit had been poured out even on the Gentiles. For they heard them speaking in tongues and praising God." *Acts 10:45, 46*

Entering the Roman amphitheatre, Caesarea.

Paul

Paul

Meaning of name: Before his conversion, Paul was called Saul; "Saul" means "asked" "Paul" means "small"

Point of interest: His conversion on the road to Damascus. "As he [Saul] neared Damascus on his journey [to persecute Christians], suddenly a light from heaven flashed around him. He fell to the ground and heard a voice say to him, 'Saul, Saul, why do you persecute me?'" *Acts 9:4.* Later Saul changed his name to Paul.

Family links: Paul was from the tribe of Benjamin and a zealous member of the Pharisee party, *Romans 11:1; Philippians 3:5; Acts 23:6.* While we know nothing about his family, we know that he was brought up in Tarsus and was a Roman citizen, *Acts 16:37; 21:39; 22:25-27.*

Old Testament link: Paul had been brought up as a devout Jew:
- " … circumcised on the eighth day,
- of the people of Israel,
- of the tribe of Benjamin,
- a Hebrew of Hebrews;
- in regard to the law, a Pharisee." *Philippians 3:5*

- Paul had been a pupil of the most respected rabbi of the day, Gamaliel, *Acts 22:3.*

Quote: Paul had an unquenchable desire to preach about Jesus: "'Woe to me if I do not preach the gospel!'" *1 Corinthians 9:16*

Link with Jesus: There is no record that Paul met Jesus while Jesus was alive. However, Paul's conversion experience was so vivid that he never forgot it as being the time when he first encountered Jesus.
"'Who are you. Lord?' Saul asked.
"'I am Jesus, whom you are persecuting,' he replied. 'Now get up and go into the city, and you will be told what you must do.'" *Acts 9:5,6*

Key verse: Paul knew that he had been forgiven for all his sins, but he never forgot that he had once persecuted Christians. "'For I am the least of the apostles and do not even deserve to be called an apostle, because I persecuted the church of God.'" *1 Corinthians 15:9*

More Information: *Acts 7, 9–28;* Paul's thirteen New Testament letters

Paul and the gospel of faith

After his conversion Paul spent the rest of his life preaching about and writing about Jesus. To the Christians at Rome Paul explained what it meant to live by faith:

"For in the gospel a righteousness from God is revealed, a righteousness that is by faith from first to last, just as it is written: 'The righteous will live by faith.'" *Romans 1:17*

Paul's physical appearance

We are told nothing about the physical appearance of Jesus or any of his apostles. It is almost the same with Paul. All we know from the New Testament are in a few verses which suggest that Paul's personal appearance was not very impressive. See *1 Corinthians 2:3-4; 2 Corinthians 10:10.*

The earliest apocryphal description of Paul says that he was, "A man small in size, bald-headed, bandy-legged, well built, with eyebrows meeting, a nose somewhat hooked, full of grace – for sometimes he seemed like a man, and sometimes he had the countenance of an angel."
Acts of Paul and Thecla
(apocryphal)

Paul's letters

After Luke, we have more writings of Paul in the New Testament than of anybody else. Thirteen letters are traditionally ascribed to Paul.

- Romans
- 1 and 2 Corinthians
- Galatians
- Ephesians
- Philippians
- Colossians
- 1 and 2 Thessalonians
- 1 and 2 Timothy
- Titus
- Philemon

Paul the pioneer missionary

Paul's missionary strategy was to take a partner or team and preach the gospel in the main cities of the known world.

"Paul stakes all his life upon the truth of what he says about the death and resurrection of Jesus." *J. Gresham Machen*

Roman coinage.

The Acropolis, Athens.

Timothy and Titus

Timothy

Meaning of name: Honoring God

Point of interest: Timothy was the apostle Paul's friend and helper.

Family links: Although Timothy's father was a Greek, Timothy was born into a strong Christian home. His mother, Eunice, was a Jew and a believer, and even his grandmother, Lois, had sincere faith in God.

Link with Jesus: In Paul's two letters to Timothy, *1 and 2 Timothy,* Paul gives Timothy advice about being a Christian leader and pastor. Timothy owed his own Christian conversion to Paul. "You then, my son, be strong in the grace that is in Christ Jesus." *2 Timothy 2:2*

Key verse: Timothy was probably shy and retiring by nature. "Don't let anyone look down on you because you are young, but set an example for the believers in speech, in life, in love, in faith and purity." *1 Timothy 4:12*

More Information: *Acts 16–17; 1 and 2 Timothy*

62

Titus

Meaning of name: Honored

Point of interest: Titus was the pastor of the Christian Church on the island of Crete.

Family links: We know nothing about Titus' family. He was one of Paul's greatly trusted friends. To some Christians who insisted that all Christians should adopt Jewish customs, Paul used Titus as an example to show how unnecessary this was. "Yet not even Titus, who was with me, was compelled to be circumcised, even though he was a Greek." *Galatians 2:3*

Words spoken about: Paul is on record as saying what a comfort Titus was to him: "But God, who comforts the downcast, comforted us by the coming of Titus." *2 Corinthians 7:6*

Link with Jesus: Paul wrote to Titus about Jesus being our Savior. See *Titus 3:6.*

Key verse: "You must teach what is in accord with sound doctrine." *Titus 2:1*

More Information: *1 Corinthians 16; 2 Corinthians 7–8; Galatians 2; the whole of Titus*

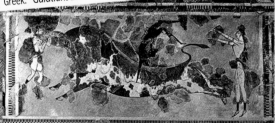

Boys and girls bull-jumping, frieze from Palace of Knossos, Crete. Minoan civilization.

Luke

Luke

Meaning of name: Light giving

Point of interest: Luke wrote the Gospel which bears his name and the Acts.

Old Testament link: Although Luke is usually thought of as being a Gentile (non-Jew) it is clear from his Gospel that he realized the great links between Jesus and the Old Testament.

In *Luke 4*, for example, Luke makes four important quotations from the Old Testament. He teaches that the whole of Jesus' ministry was foretold by Isaiah, as he records Jesus reading from *Isaiah 61:1-2*, after which Jesus said, "'Today this scripture is fulfilled in your hearing.'" *Luke 4:21*

Quote: Luke explains why he wrote his Gospel in its opening verses: "Therefore, since I myself have carefully investigated everything from the beginning, it seemed good also to me to write an orderly account for you, most excellent Theophilus, so that you may know the certainty of the things you have been taught." *Luke 1:3, 4*

Link with Jesus: Luke records 17 of Jesus' parables which are not found in the other three Gospels. The most famous two of these are the Good Samaritan and the Prodigal Son. See *Luke 10:30-37; 15:11-32*.

Key verse: Luke summed up Jesus' mission in the following words of Jesus: "For the Son of Man came to seek and to save what was lost." *Luke 19:10*

More Information: *Colossians 4:2 Timothy 4;* the books of *Luke* and *Acts*

Luke the faithful doctor

As Paul's traveling companion, Luke was greatly appreciated. In *Colossians 4:14* Paul calls Luke, "Our dear friend Luke, the doctor." That Paul prized Luke's faithful friendship is seen in some of the last words Paul wrote: "Only Luke is with me." *2 Timothy 4:11*

Index of Bible people